SHOWSTOPPERS
Playalong *for* Saxophone

D1514472

WISE PUBLICATIONS
London/New York/Paris/Sydney/Copenhagen/Madrid

Exclusive Distributors:
Music Sales Limited
8/9 Frith Street, London W1V 5TZ, England.
Music Sales Pty Limited
120 Rothschild Avenue, Rosebery, NSW 2018, Australia.

Order No. AM941842
ISBN 0-7119-6276-6
This book © Copyright 1998 by Wise Publications.

Book design by Michael Bell Design.
Compiled by Peter Evans.
Music arranged by Jack Long.
Music processed by Enigma Music Production Services.
Cover photography by George Taylor.
CD recorded by Paul Honey.
Instrumental solos by John Whelan.
All keyboards and programming by Paul Honey.

Printed in the United Kingdom by
Page Bros Ltd, Norwich, Norfolk.

Your Guarantee of Quality:
As publishers, we strive to produce every book to
the highest commercial standards.
The music has been freshly engraved and the book has been
carefully designed to minimise awkward page turns and
to make playing from it a real pleasure.
Particular care has been given to specifying acid-free, neutral-sized
paper made from pulps which have not been elemental chlorine bleached.
This pulp is from farmed sustainable forests and was
produced with special regard for the environment.
Throughout, the printing and binding have been planned to
ensure a sturdy, attractive publication which should give years of enjoyment.
If your copy fails to meet our high standards,
please inform us and we will gladly replace it.

Music Sales' complete catalogue describes thousands of
titles and is available in full colour sections by subject,
direct from Music Sales Limited.
Please state your areas of interest and send a
cheque/postal order for £1.50 for postage to:
Music Sales Limited, Newmarket Road, Bury St. Edmunds, Suffolk IP33 3YB.

Visit the Internet Music Shop at
http://www.musicsales.co.uk

Big Spender 23
Sweet Charity

Bring Him Home 18
Les Misérables

Don't Cry For Me Argentina 9
Evita

I Don't Know How To Love Him 16
Jesus Christ Superstar

I Dreamed A Dream 20
Les Misérables

I Know Him So Well 6
Chess

If I Were A Rich Man 12
Fiddler On The Roof

Maria 26
West Side Story

Somewhere 28
West Side Story

Tonight 30
West Side Story

Fingering Guide 4

Fingering Guide

Transposition

The B♭ soprano saxophone sounds a major second below the written pitch.
Rule: Written C sounds B♭

The B♭ tenor saxophone sounds a major ninth below the written pitch.
Rule: Written C sounds B♭

The E♭ alto saxophone sounds a major sixth below the written pitch.
Rule: Written C sounds E♭

The E♭ baritone saxophone sounds an octave plus a major sixth below the written pitch.
Rule: Written C sounds E♭

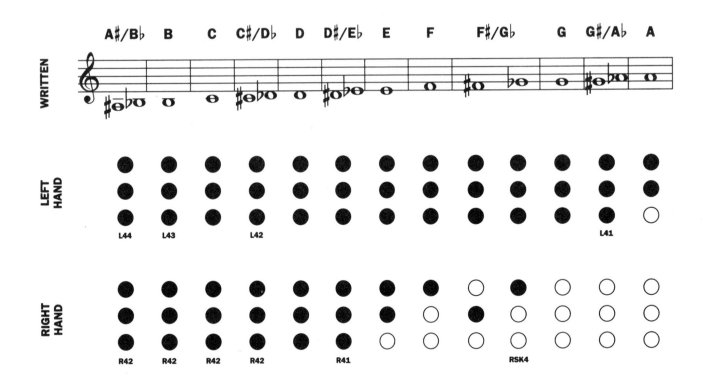

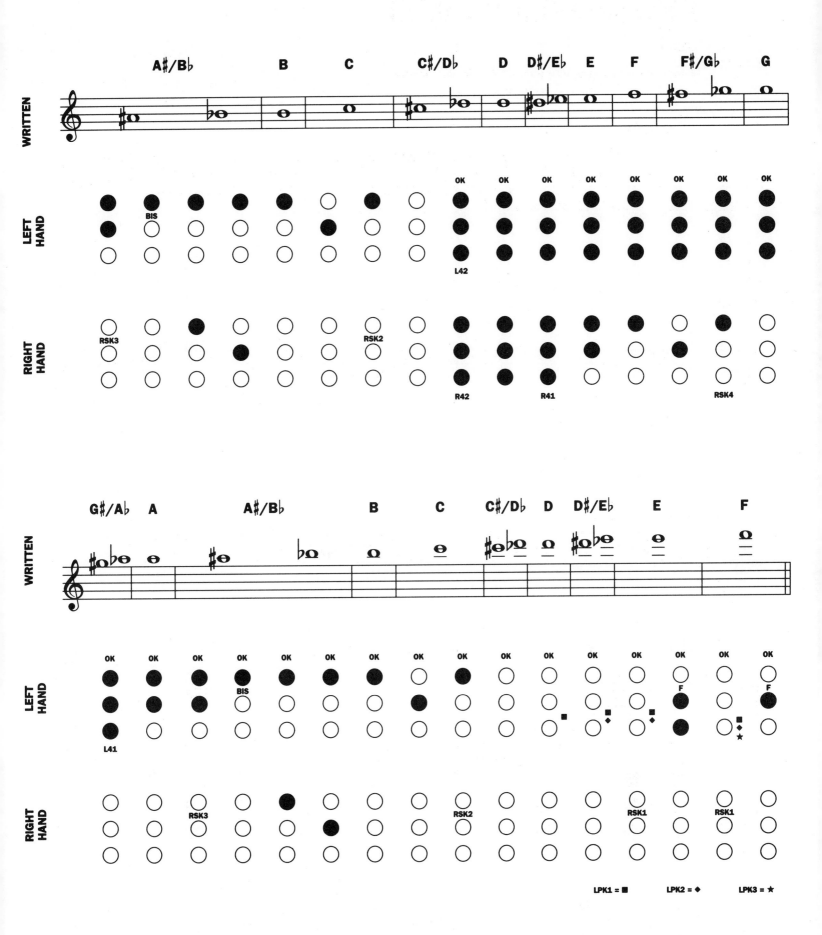

I Know Him So Well

Chess

Words & Music by Benny Andersson, Tim Rice & Bjorn Ulvaeus

Medium slow (♩ = 70)

dim.

mp

Don't Cry For Me Argentina

Evita

Music by Andrew Lloyd Webber
Lyrics by Tim Rice

If I Were A Rich Man

Fiddler On The Roof

Words by Sheldon Harnick
Music by Jerry Bock

Moderate '2' ($\quarternote$ = 122)

$\oplus$ **CODA**

Slower

Tempo 1

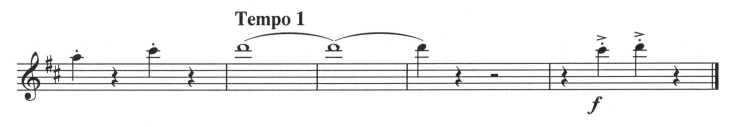

f

I Don't Know How To Love Him

Jesus Christ Superstar

Music by Andrew Lloyd Webber
Lyrics by Tim Rice

Bring Him Home

From The Musical 'Les Misérables'

Music by Claude-Michel Schönberg
Lyric by Herbert Kretzmer & Alain Boublil

Slow (♩ = 69)

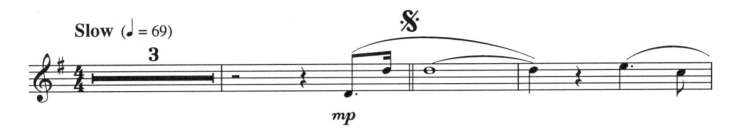

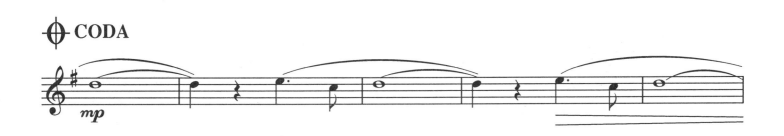

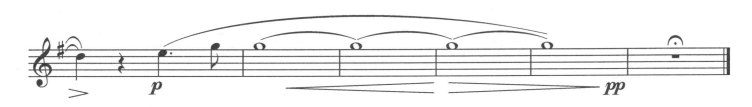

I Dreamed A Dream

From The Musical 'Les Misérables'

Music by Claude-Michel Schönberg
Lyric by Herbert Kretzmer
Original Text by Alain Boublil & Jean-Marc Natel

Slow (♩ = c. 64)

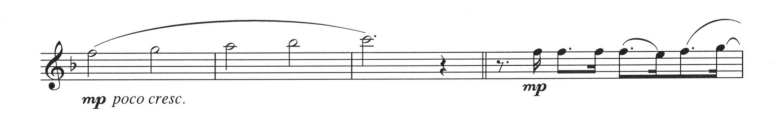

Big Spender

Sweet Charity

Words by Dorothy Fields
Music by Cy Coleman

'Stripper' Tempo (♩. = 112)

D. 𝄋 al Coda

CODA

mf

f

Maria

West Side Story

Music by Leonard Bernstein
Lyrics by Stephen Sondheim

Somewhere

West Side Story

Music by Leonard Bernstein.
Lyrics by Stephen Sondheim

Medium slow (♩ = 76)

Tonight

West Side Story

Music by Leonard Bernstein
Lyrics by Stephen Sondheim

Moderate 'Beguine' tempo (♩ = 120)

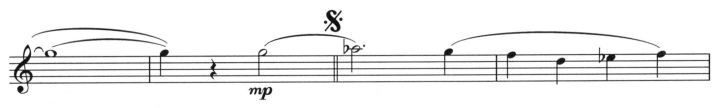

⊕ CODA

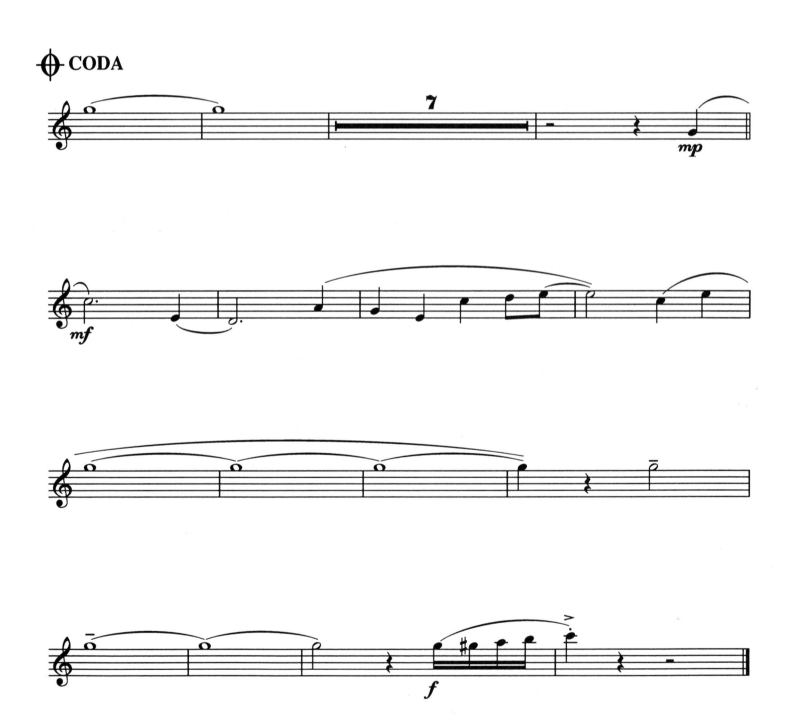

9/98 (31989)